COOL PETS for Kids

Horses and Ponies

DAWN TITMUS

PowerKiDS press

Published in 2019 by The Rosen
Publishing Group, Inc.
29 East 21st Street, New York, NY 10010

Cataloging-in-Publication Data

Names: Titmus, Dawn.
Title: Horses and ponies / Dawn Titmus.
Description: New York : PowerKids Press, 2019. | Series: Cool pets for kids | Includes glossary and index.
Identifiers: LCCN ISBN 9781538337981 (pbk.) | ISBN 9781538337974 (library bound) |
ISBN 9781538337998 (6 pack)
Subjects: LCSH: Horses--Juvenile literature. | Ponies--Juvenile literature. | Pets--Juvenile literature.
Classification: LCC SF302.T58 2019 | DDC 636.1--dc23

Text and editor: Dawn Titmus
Editorial Director: Lindsey Lowe
Children's Publisher: Anne O'Daly
Design Manager: Keith Davis
Picture Manager: Sophie Mortimer

Photo acknowledgements:
t=top, c=center, b=bottom, l=left, r=right
Interior: Alamy: Angela Hampton Picture Library 13r, ImageBROKER 27t; Dreamstime: Pat Olson 9b; Getty
Images: Dorling Kindersley 26–27, Lea Roth 24–25; iStock: Anna Elizabeth Photography 16, capnap72 27b,
Caziopela 25b, cynoclub 7bl, GlobalIP 18–19b, 22–23, Groomee 17, Gurr Photography 21b, mari_art 23t,
matthewleesdixon 29t, Mlenny 18–19t, Marilyn Nieves 9t, olgaIT 14, Picture Partners 8b, Roxanne Roy 21t,
tunart 19, wavebreakmedia 16–17; Shutterstock: anakondasp 8t, Marie Charouzova 29b, cynoclub 4–5, 7br,
Ewais 6–7, Fotokostic 15b, Fragolini 25t, Bianca Grueneberg 10–11, Eric Isselee 3, Grigorita Ko 29c, Iofio69
18, lucag_g 23b, Sari O'Neal 6bl, 10, Maralee Park 7bc, pirita 12r, 13l, purplequeue 1, racorn 12l, Vasyl Syniuk
4, Ad van Brunschot 6br, wavebreakmedia 11, 15t, Vera Zinkova 20–21.

Manufactured in the United States of America

CPSIA Compliance Information: Batch #CS18PK: For Further Information contact Rosen Publishing, New York,
New York at 1-800-237-9932.

Contents

Which Horse or Pony?

Looking after a horse or pony can be lots of fun. They are intelligent animals and will be great companions, but they need a lot of care.

Horse or Pony?

The height of a horse or pony is measured in hands. One hand equals 4 inches (10 cm). Usually, ponies are smaller than 14.5 hands, or 58 inches (1.47 m). Horses and ponies can live for 30 years.

Time and Energy

Looking after a horse or pony takes time and effort. They need to be fed, watered, groomed, and exercised every day. Horses and ponies also need visits from the vet and farrier. Think carefully about whether you have the time and energy to spare.

Paddock or Stable?

Horses and ponies need plenty of space to graze and roam. You will need to provide shelter, too. If you have a paddock, you may choose to keep your pet at home. Another option is to pay to keep your horse at a stable.

The Right Pet for You?

☑ Do you have space for a horse or pony?

☑ Do you have time to look after and exercise a horse or pony every day?

☑ Can your family afford to keep a horse or pony?

Your Budget

It is costly to keep a horse or pony. As well as feed and stabling, you will need equipment for grooming and riding. There will also be vet and farrier bills to pay.

Read On ...

Horses and ponies make great pets, but it is important to think carefully before owning one. This book describes the basics of caring for horses and ponies, and looks at four popular breeds. Make a "stained glass" horse window. You will also find some fascinating facts about our equine friends!

What You Will Need

You will need lots of different equipment to care for your horse properly. Grooming tools are essential to keep your horse clean. You will also need riding gear and perhaps barn equipment.

Checklist

- ☑ Grooming brushes and combs.
- ☑ Hoof pick.
- ☑ Feed tub and water bucket.
- ☑ Cleaning equipment for the barn.
- ☑ Tack: halter, lead rope, saddle, saddle pad, and bridle.
- ☑ Hard helmet, riding boots, and gloves.

Grooming Kit

Different types of brushes and combs are used for grooming a horse. The mane and tail need to be groomed regularly. Special brushes and combs are used to polish the horse's coat. You will also need a hoof pick to remove stones from the hooves.

Dandy brush

Hoof pick

Mane and tail brush, and comb

Barn Equipment

If you keep your pet at home, you will need a feed tub and water trough or buckets, as well as hay nets or hay racks. The stall has to be cleaned out regularly, so you will also need a pitchfork, stable broom, wheelbarrow, and manure fork.

Riding Gear and Tack

Your horse will need a well-fitting saddle, saddle pad or blanket, and a bridle. Western saddles are bigger and heavier than English saddles. English saddles have metal stirrups, while Western saddles have leather ones. Always wear a helmet when riding. You also need boots that have at least a 1-inch (2.5 cm) heel to stop your feet from slipping through the stirrups. Wearing gloves protects your hands and prevents the reins from slipping.

Hard helmet

Riding gloves

English saddle

Western saddle

Bridle

Riding boots

Stirrup

Staying Safe

Using the right equipment and being sensible around horses and ponies will keep you safe. Take your time and follow some basic safety rules.

Clothing and Tack

When you ride, always wear a helmet and boots with a heel to stop your feet from slipping through the stirrups. Wearing gloves helps prevent the reins slipping in your hands. Wear hard-toed boots around horses. A horse stepping on your foot will hurt! Clean the tack regularly and check it is safe.

Leading and Tying

Learn how to put a halter and rope on a horse safely. Ask an experienced rider to show you if you're not sure. When leading a horse, walk by its neck or shoulder. To turn the horse, turn it away from you and walk around it. Never wrap the lead rope around your hand or arm. If your horse suddenly pulls, your hand or arm may become trapped. If you need to tether, or tie up, your horse while you groom it, tie it to a tie ring or strong post.

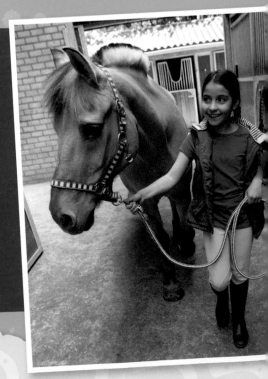

Check Equipment

Check that the equipment you're using is not worn or broken. Look for fraying lead ropes or halters that could break when your horse is tied up. Always check the girth is secured properly before you mount your horse. If it's loose, the saddle may slip and you could fall off!

Horse Language

Learn to understand your pet's body language. A horse that is swishing its tail or turning its rump toward you is showing it is unhappy and may kick. Horses have blind spots right in front and behind them. Touch a horse on its shoulder or neck, not its nose. Never surprise a horse or approach it from behind. It may kick if it's surprised. When grooming the tail, stand to the side of the horse, not right behind it. Let it know what you're doing by touching it firmly and talking to it. Be calm and never get angry with a horse or pony.

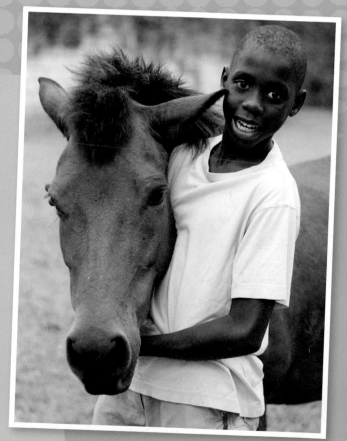

Feeding Time

Horses and ponies need a well-balanced diet to stay fit and healthy. Their stomachs are small, so they feed little and often.

Fresh Water

Horses need plenty of fresh water. They can drink from 10 to 12 gallons (38 to 45 liters) of water in one day. If you live in an area with cold winters, you can use a water heater or heated buckets to keep ice from forming on drinking water.

Eats Like a Horse!

Horses eat a lot! The average-sized horse eats about 15 to 20 pounds (7 to 9.5 kg) of food every day. Exactly how much your horse needs depends on its size and how much activity it does. A horse that is not being ridden or worked needs less food than a very active horse, such as a racehorse.

Hay and Grain

Feed your horse or pony at least three times a day. Their diet should be mainly forage, such as alfalfa, grass hay, or pasture. The natural food of horses and ponies is grass. Many horses get all they need to eat just from grazing in a pasture. Stall horses need to have hay to munch on. Most horses also need grain. Grain is made from oats, corn, bran, or barley. Give your horse small amounts of grain frequently rather than one large meal.

Poison

Some plants are poisonous for horses. Plants such as yew, bracken fern, dogbane, and milkweed should be removed from your horse's pasture. Contact your county extension office for information about which poisonous plants grow in your county.

Grooming and Cleaning

Grooming your horse every day will keep its coat sleek and shiny. Your horse's stall also needs cleaning out at least once a day.

Daily Grooming

Make sure your horse is safely tied up. Clean out the hooves using a hoof pick. Use a curry comb or mitt to remove dead hair and dirt from the coat moving with strong, circular strokes. This massages the skin and releases natural oils, making the coat shine. Use a dandy brush to flick off the dirt, then finish off with a body brush to make the coat glossy.

Mane and Tail

The mane and tail can become tangled. Use a brush or comb to gently tease out the tangles, or use your fingers to detangle before you start brushing. Begin at the end of the tail and work your way up. Stand to the side so you can't get kicked. Grooming sprays can also help untangle mane and tail hair.

Finishing Touches

Use a damp sponge or soft cloth to gently clean your horse's ears, eyes, and nose. Check the ears for dirt or grass seeds. Go slowly, as some horses don't like their ears being touched. Finally, use the cloth or sponge to clean the area under the tail, standing to the side so you don't get kicked.

Cleaning the Stall

Use a pitchfork or shovel to remove manure and wet bedding every day. Replace the soiled bedding with clean bedding. Sweep up straw or wood shavings. Completely clean out the stall once a week and replace all the bedding.

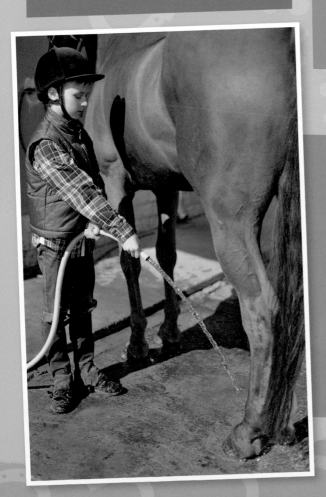

Bath Time

If you are taking your horse to a show, wash it a few days before the event. It will give the coat time to get its glossy sheen back. Use a small amount of special shampoo. Be careful not to spray water directly into your horse's face! Dry your horse with a sweat scraper and towels, then walk it around for a few minutes to finish drying, or cover it with a thin blanket.

Shelter and Exercise

All horses and ponies need some protection from the weather and somewhere to exercise. You can exercise your horse by riding, driving, or longeing. The type of shelter they need depends on where they live.

Outdoor Pasture

If your horse or pony lives on outdoor pasture, it can exercise as much as it likes. Horses are naturally herd animals, so it will be happier if there are other horses on the same pasture. They will need shelter from the sun in summer and from the wind, rain, and cold in winter. A small three-sided shed should provide them with enough shelter.

Indoor Stall

The size of the stall you need depends on the size of your horse or pony. Most horses will be happy in a stall that is 12 by 10 feet (3.5 by 3 m). Ponies are comfortable in smaller stalls. Horses that live in a stall need to be exercised every day. You can turn your horse out to pasture or a paddock for exercise. Follow this with at least one hour a day of riding, driving, or longeing.

Paddock Horse

Some horses live in a pen or paddock. A paddock is a small field or pasture. A pen is an outside space that should ideally be at least 24 by 24 feet (7.3 by 7.3 m). Horses in a large pen or paddock can exercise by themselves, but they will need to have some extra exercise three or four times a week.

Staying Healthy

Help your horse or pony stay healthy by feeding it the right foods and giving it plenty of exercise. But just like people, horses and ponies will get sick sometimes.

Daily Checks

Knowing how your horse behaves when it's healthy helps you spot the signs when it's sick. A healthy horse looks alert with bright eyes and holds the ears forward. Grooming is a good time to check for any lumps or injuries on your horse. Notice how it is standing. A horse holding up a leg may be lame. Does your horse limp when it moves or take small steps? Call the vet if you think your horse may be lame.

Hoof Care

Check your horse's hooves every day for dirt or loose shoes. Like fingernails, hooves keep growing. They will need to be trimmed by a farrier every six to eight weeks. Don't let your horse stand in water or a wet stall for long. Wet hooves may split and break.

Signs of Sickness

- ✅ Your pet is not eating its food or drinking water.
- ✅ Its eyes are dull or it looks nervous.
- ✅ It is rolling around on the ground (colic).
- ✅ It is limping or taking small, awkward steps (lameness).

Parasites

All horses have worms that live inside their bodies. Most horses need a deworming treatment every two months. Watch out for tiny yellow botfly eggs on your horse. Remove the eggs with a bot block or a blunt pocket knife. Also have your vet check your horse for ticks and lice.

Colic

Horses and ponies cannot throw up if they eat poison or too much food. They get a bad stomachache, called colic, if something has upset their stomach. Your pet might have colic if it is restless, lying down and rolling over, or looking at its sides. Call the vet if you think your pet has colic.

In the Wild

Horses and ponies belong to the same family as asses, donkeys, and zebras. Wild horses once lived all over the world. About 6,000 years ago, people domesticated horses.

Przewalski's Horse

Przewalski's horse comes from Mongolia and China. It became extinct in the wild. Some horses were kept and bred in captivity. They were set free in nature reserves in Mongolia and China. Today, there are about 2,000 Przewalski's horses in reserves in Asia and Europe.

Mustangs and Brumbies

Mustangs (left) and brumbies are feral horses. They are descended from domestic horses that were turned loose or escaped into the wild. Mustangs are descended from Spanish horses that were introduced to the Americas in the 1500s. Brumbies live in Australia. They are descended from horses the British first took to Australia in 1788.

Herds of Horses

Horses live in herds in the wild. Usually, there is a stallion with a group of mares and their foals. When colts are about two or three years old, the stallion drives them away from the herd. The colts may band together until they start their own herds.

Semiwild Horse

Some horses are semiwild. They have owners but are left to roam free most of the time. Shetland ponies (left) live semiwild on the Shetland Islands, off the north coast of Scotland. Camargue horses in southern France have a semiwild life. Semiwild horses also live in England, Germany, and Norway.

Quarter Horse

The American quarter horse is the most popular breed in the United States. Its name comes from the fact that it was faster than other horse breeds in races of a quarter mile (400 m) or less.

Where in the World?

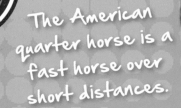

The American quarter horse was first bred by settlers in the 1800s in what is now the United States. In the American West, the quarter horse was used as a ranch horse by cowboys and as a racing horse.

The American quarter horse is a fast horse over short distances.

Breed Profile

The quarter horse stands between 14.3 and 16 hands high. It comes in a range of colors, including bay, chestnut, and white. It has a strong, muscular body and excels in rodeo events. Quarter horses can live for up to 30 years.

Looking After Me

Quarter horses are excellent riding, race, and show horses. They are suited to owners who have limited experience.

- ☑ Quarter horses do well on a simple diet of hay.

- ☑ Don't overfeed your pet. Quarter horses put on weight easily.

Appaloosa

The Appaloosa is instantly recognizable from its coat of dark or white spots. It is a strong, gentle, intelligent animal.

The leopard spot Appaloosa has spots all over its body.

Where in the World?

The Nez Perce Native Americans first bred Appaloosas in the 1700s. The Appaloosa was recognized as a breed in 1938. It is the state horse of Idaho.

Breed Profile

Appaloosas stand between 14.2 and 15.2 hands high. They can have spots over all of their body or part of it. They have striped hooves, and the whites of their eyes are visible. The base coat comes in a range of colors, including black, bay, and gray. The Appaloosa can live for up to 30 years.

Looking After Me

Appaloosas are usually calm and reliable. They are considered to be good horses for children to ride.

- ☑ They can live happily on pasture or in a barn or box stall.

- ☑ Appaloosas can be prone to sunburn. Use a good sunblock on pink or white areas of their muzzle.

Connemara Pony

Connemara ponies are strong and agile. They are also intelligent and have calm, gentle natures. The breed is a good first pony for children.

Where in the World?

The Connemara pony comes from the Connemara region in western Ireland. Irish farmers used them to pull plows and haul heavy loads up until the 1950s.

The Connemara pony is agile and good at jumping.

Breed Profile

Connemaras stand from 12.2 to 14.2 hands high. They are one of the largest pony breeds. It is muscular, and its coat is usually gray or brown, but it can be cream or black. Connemaras have long manes and tails. They can live for more than 30 years.

Looking After Me

The Connemara is often used in dressage and long-distance riding. It is a natural jumper.

- ☑ An "easy keeper," it is happy living outdoors all year round. It can eat a simple diet of hay and does not need grain.

- ☑ Connemaras can suffer with lameness. Keep an eye out and call the vet if your pony is limping.

Pony of the Americas

The Pony of the Americas is one of the largest ponies. It looks more like a small horse.

The Pony of the Americas is strong and fast.

Where in the World?

The Pony of the Americas was first bred in Iowa in 1954 from an Arabian/Appaloosa mare and a Shetland stallion. It was originally bred for working with livestock.

Breed Profile

The Pony of the Americas stands from 11.2 to 14 hands high. It has a wide range of coat patterns, the most common being the blanket pattern. This is white over the back part of the pony's body with dark spots. The spots may be tiny or more than 4 inches (10 cm) wide. Some ponies have spotting over the whole body. This is called the leopard pattern. The Pony of the Americas can live for up to 30 years.

Looking After Me

This pony is a good all-arounder and performs well in equesrian sports such as rodeo events.

- ☑ Pink nose areas can become sunburned, so use sunblock in hot weather.

- ☑ Groom regularly to keep white coats in good condition.

Make It!

Horse Window

Use colored tissue paper and construction paper to make a "stained glass" window with a horse's head for your bedroom.

You Will Need:

Scissors
Waxed paper
Colored tissue paper
Glue
Black construction paper
Tape (optional)

1 Find a picture of a solid black horse head. You can find one online with an adult's permission.

2 Print the horse head and carefully cut it out.

3 Cut out a piece of waxed paper that is large enough for your horse head to fit onto.

4 Tear colored tissue paper into long strips or small squares.

5 Glue the tissue paper onto the waxed paper. Overlap the pieces to make a pretty background.

6 Put the horse head on top of the tissue paper. When you are happy with the position, glue it in place.

7 Cut four strips of black construction paper to make a frame for your window. Glue or tape the corners together. Then glue the strips around your window.

Put your window in front of a light or tape it onto your bedroom window so the light shines through.

Did You Know?

Horses use their ears, eyes, and nostrils to show how they feel. They sniff each other's noses to say hello. They also express their feelings through their tail. Swishing the tail up and down can mean that the horse is annoyed.

Horses have a better sense of hearing than humans. They can turn their ears around toward sounds coming from different directions.

Horses use different sounds to communicate. They whinny or neigh when they meet or leave another horse. Stallions roar loudly when they are seeking a mate. Horses snort to warn other horses of danger.

Usually, horses in a herd don't all lie down at the same time. At least one horse stays standing to be lookout and warn the others of any danger.

In the United States, there are about 1.75 million workhorses. Among other jobs, they work on farms, in rodeos, and with police.

Horses have almost 360-degree vision. They have blind spots directly in front and behind them.

Horses' teeth keep growing and are worn down by chewing. The shape and angle of a horse's teeth change as it ages. Vets can estimate a horse's age by looking at the shape and angle of its teeth.

Horses are used in therapy. Interacting with a horse helps people build trust and self-confidence, improve communication, and learn new skills.

Glossary

alfalfa plant grown for hay.

blind spot area that the eye cannot see.

bot block rough stone used to remove botfly eggs from horse's hair.

botfly type of fly that lives inside some mammals before it becomes adult and can fly.

captivity the state of being kept by people, not free.

colt young male horse.

descended comes from the same family.

domesticated living with people.

dominant controlling others.

dressage show event in which horses make special movements in response to riders' signals.

driving (of horses) pulling a cart or carriage.

equestrian relating to riding.

equine relating to horses.

farrier person who cares for and shoes horses' hooves.

feral describes an animal that has escaped and become wild.

forage grasses and other plants eaten by animals.

girth strap to hold a saddle on a horse's back.

lice small insects that live on the bodies of animals and people.

longeing exercising a horse on a long rein or strap.

mare female horse.

muzzle jaws and nose of an animal.

paddock small field where animals are kept.

stallion male horse.

sweat scraper tool to remove lather from a sweating horse.

tick very small insect that attaches itself to a larger animal and feeds on it.

Further Resources

Books

Henderson, Carolyn.
The Pony Club Guide to Caring for a Horse or Pony, Quiller, 2015.

Lomberg, Michelle.
Horse (Caring for My Pet), AV2 by Weigl, 2016.

Lowenstein, Felicia Niven.
Learning to Care for a Horse (Beginning Pet Care with American Humane), Enslow Publishers, Inc., 2010.

Websites

Due to the changing nature of Internet links, PowerKids Press has developed an online list of websites related to the subject of this book. This site is updated regularly. Please use this link to access the list:

www.powerkidslinks.com/cpfk/horses

Index